GREEK MYTHOLOGY

PEGASUS

BY WHITNEY SANDERSON

CONTENT CONSULTANT
MARK THORNE, PhD
ASSISTANT PROFESSOR OF CLASSICS
LUTHER COLLEGE

Kids Core

An Imprint of Abdo Publishing
abdobooks.com

abdobooks.com

Published by Abdo Publishing, a division of ABDO, PO Box 398166, Minneapolis, Minnesota 55439. Copyright © 2022 by Abdo Consulting Group, Inc. International copyrights reserved in all countries. No part of this book may be reproduced in any form without written permission from the publisher. Kids Core™ is a trademark and logo of Abdo Publishing.

Printed in the United States of America, North Mankato, Minnesota.
102021
012022

Cover Photos: Voropaev Vasiliy/Shutterstock Images, (Pegasus); Shutterstock Images, (background)
Interior Photos: Shutterstock Images, 4–5, 25, 28 (bottom), 29 (top); Steve Estvanik/Shutterstock Images, 6; iStockphoto, 8, 20; Alex Mastro/Shutterstock Images, 9, 29 (bottom); Lambros Kazan/Shutterstock Images, 10; Dea/A. Dagliorti/De Agostini/Getty Images, 12–13; Pavle Marjanovic/Shutterstock Images, 15; Juniors Bildarchiv GmbH/Alamy, 16, 28 (top); Mondadori Portfolio//Hulton Fine Art Collection/Getty Images, 19; Tanya Keisha/Shutterstock Images, 22–23; Mihai Andritoiu/Alamy, 26

Editor: Alyssa Sorenson
Series Designer: Ryan Gale

Library of Congress Control Number: 2021941213
Publisher's Cataloging-in-Publication Data

Names: Sanderson, Whitney, author.
Title: Pegasus / by Whitney Sanderson
Description: Minneapolis, Minnesota : Abdo Publishing, 2022 | Series: Greek mythology | Includes online resources and index.
Identifiers: ISBN 9781532196799 (lib. bdg.) | ISBN 9781098218607 (ebook)
Subjects: LCSH: Pegasus (Greek mythology)--Juvenile literature. | Animals, Mythical--Juvenile literature. | Mythology, Greek--Juvenile literature. | Gods, Greek--Juvenile literature.
Classification: DDC 292--dc23

CONTENTS

CHAPTER 1
A Winged Hero 4

CHAPTER 2
The Life of Pegasus 12

CHAPTER 3
Pegasus in the Stars 22

Legendary Facts 28
Glossary 30
Online Resources 31
Learn More 31
Index 32
About the Author 32

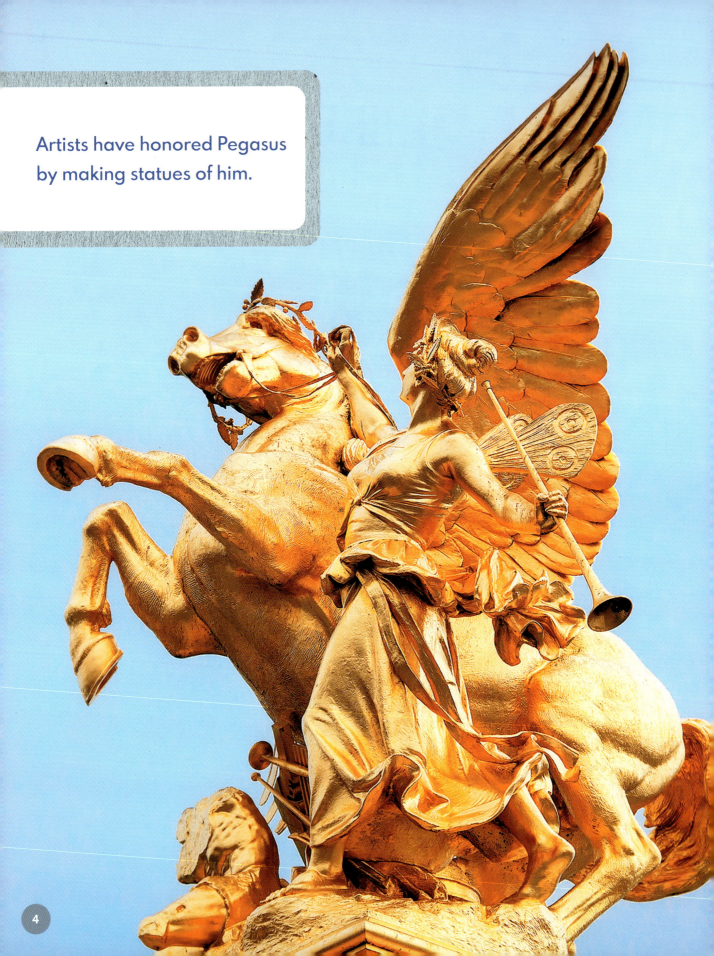

Artists have honored Pegasus by making statues of him.

CHAPTER 1

A WINGED HERO

A shining horse soared through the sky. Every beat of Pegasus's wings carried him closer to his destination. His sharp eyes spotted what looked like bonfires burning the landscape below. Pegasus's nostrils filled with the smell of smoke.

With Pegasus's help, Bellerophon was able to face the Chimera.

Pegasus felt the weight of Bellerophon on his back. Bellerophon was a hero. The king of Lycia had sent him here on a **quest**. He had to kill a fire-breathing Chimera. The monster had been burning the countryside.

As Pegasus got closer to the ground, he saw the Chimera. The creature had the head of a lion. Its middle part looked like a goat. The back of its body resembled a snake. The **fearsome** monster had destroyed many areas in Lycia. It seemed no one could defeat it.

Ancient Cities

The ancient Greeks were neighbors with many other **civilizations**. One of these was Lycia. The region was in what is now the country of Turkey. Some coins from Lycia have images of Pegasus on them.

Many artists have imagined how Pegasus and Bellerophon beat the Chimera.

The Chimera was a strong and fierce opponent.

Bellerophon took out his bow. He started firing arrows at the monster. Pegasus beat his wings to keep them in the air. He dodged the Chimera's flames. Soon, the Chimera slowed down. Bellerophon kept attacking. Eventually the Chimera fell to the ground and lay still. Pegasus and Bellerophon had done what nobody else could. They had killed the monster.

Some ancient buildings are still in Greece today.

The Ancient Greeks

Ancient Greece was a **civilization** in southeastern Europe. It existed more than 2,000 years ago. The ancient Greeks worshipped many different gods and goddesses. They made buildings called temples. Inside were statues of the gods. People worshipped different gods for different reasons, such as to help crops grow or to bring good luck in battle. The stories Greeks told about their gods and goddesses are called myths. These myths are filled with fantastic animals, such as Pegasus.

> ## Further Evidence
>
> Visit the website below. Does it give any new information to support Chapter One?
>
> ### Five Terrifying Tales from Greek Mythology
>
> abdocorelibrary.com/pegasus

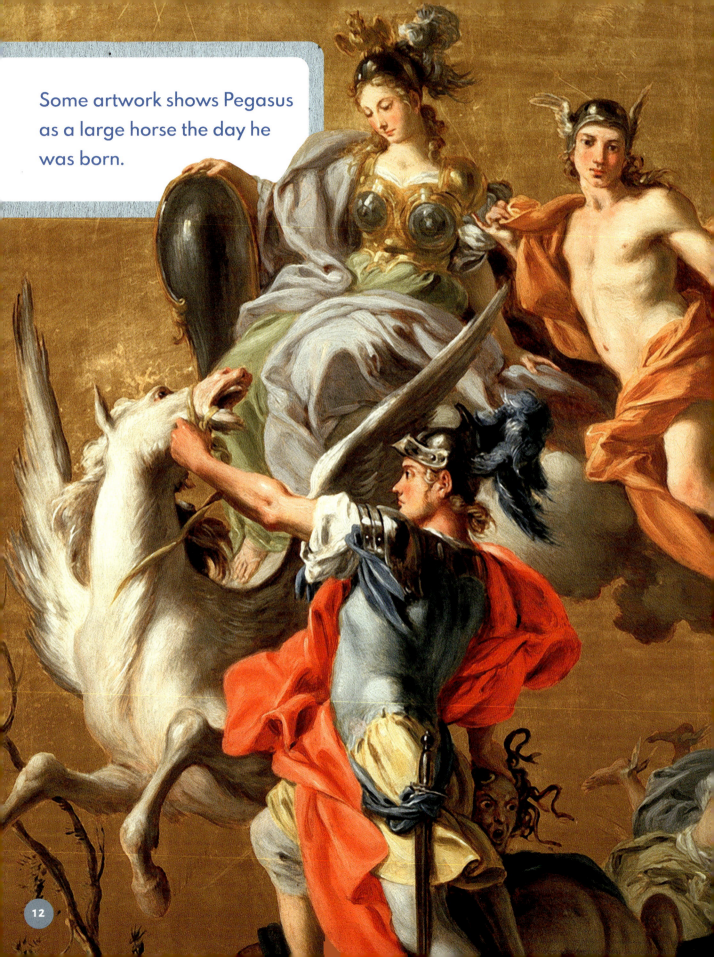

Some artwork shows Pegasus as a large horse the day he was born.

CHAPTER **2**

THE LIFE OF PEGASUS

Pegasus's father was the sea god Poseidon. His mother was Medusa, a snake-headed monster. Pegasus was born after a hero named Perseus killed Medusa. Then Pegasus leapt from her body.

Pegasus was nothing like his mother. He was a horse with wings. He had more in common with his father. Poseidon was the god of horses, the sea, and earthquakes. Pegasus also had some power over water. He could create springs by hitting the ground with his hooves.

Pegasus was said to have created a spring called the Hippocrene on Mount Helicon. Nine goddesses called the Muses lived there. Drinking water from the Hippocrene **inspired** the Muses to create art and music. Although the story is a myth, Mount Helicon is a real place in Greece.

Each Muse was in charge of a different art form. For example, Terpsichore was in charge of lyric poetry and dance.

The ancient Greeks believed Pegasus was immortal. That meant he could not die.

Pegasus Tamed

Pegasus lived free in the wilderness. No one could tell him what to do. But Bellerophon wanted to tame Pegasus. He needed the winged horse to fight the Chimera. Bellerophon went to the goddess Athena's temple. He asked for help. Athena visited Bellerophon in a dream. She gave him a golden **bridle**. She said it would allow him to ride Pegasus. When Bellerophon woke up, the bridle was sitting beside him.

A Hero's Journey

In Greek myths, heroes are people who do extraordinary things. They sometimes have special powers. They are not gods, but heroes are often related to gods or goddesses. Greek myths about heroes often center around dangerous journeys or tasks, such as Bellerophon slaying the Chimera.

Bellerophon sneaked up on Pegasus while the horse was drinking from a spring. The hero slipped the golden bridle onto Pegasus's head. Now the flying horse knew Bellerophon was worthy to ride him. After they defeated the Chimera, they battled other enemies across the kingdom. Pegasus and Bellerophon had many adventures together.

A Dangerous Journey

Bellerophon grew very proud. He began to think he was equal to the gods. He decided to fly with Pegasus to Mount Olympus, where the gods lived. Zeus was the king there. He was angry. He sent a fly to sting Pegasus.

Some stories say Pegasus and Bellerophon also fought humans together, not just monsters.

The myth of Pegasus knocking off Bellerophon is a warning for humans to not become too proud or greedy.

After Pegasus was stung, he began to buck in the air. Bellerophon was thrown from his back. The hero fell to the ground far below. He never finished his journey.

Pegasus continued to Mount Olympus alone. Zeus welcomed him. He stabled Pegasus with the other horses of the gods. Pegasus was given the honor of carrying Zeus's thunderbolts.

PRIMARY SOURCE

Hesiod was a Greek poet who lived in the 700s BCE. He wrote about Pegasus in a poem:

> With [Medusa] lay the Dark-haired One [Poseidon]. . . . And when Perseus cut off [Medusa's] head, there sprang forth . . . the horse Pegasus. . . . Pegasus flew away and left the earth . . . and he dwells in the house of Zeus and brings to wise Zeus the thunder and lightning.

Source: "Hesiod, *Theogony*, Line 270." *Perseus Digital Library*, n.d., perseus.tufts.edu. Accessed 11 May 2021.

Comparing Texts

Does the poem support the information in this chapter? Or does it give a different perspective? Explain how in a few sentences.

Pegasus may be one of the most recognizable figures in Greek mythology.

CHAPTER 3

PEGASUS IN THE STARS

The Greeks had stories of how Zeus wanted to honor Pegasus. He created a **constellation** of stars in the shape of a flying horse. Then whenever people looked up at the night sky, they would see Pegasus and remember his brave deeds.

In the Northern Hemisphere, the Pegasus constellation is clearest in the fall months. A group of four stars called the Great Square of Pegasus is the easiest part to find. The brightest star in Pegasus is called Enif, or Epsilon Pegasi. It marks Pegasus's nose. Pegasus looks upside down in the sky. His neck and head are below his hooves.

A Symbol of Strength

During World War II (1939–1945), the British Airborne Forces used an image of Pegasus and Bellerophon as its badge. People saw it as a **symbol** of power.

The Pegasus Constellation

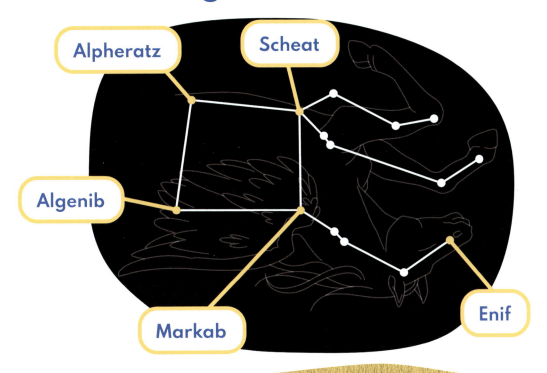

The Pegasus constellation doesn't look much like a horse. Instead, it looks like a large box with legs. But the shape of this constellation is very recognizable. Some people think it's easy to find in the night sky if you know where the main stars in the constellation are.

Pegasus throughout History

The stories of Pegasus inspired people in ancient Greece. He was a **symbol** of beauty.

Ancient artwork showing Pegasus keeps his legend alive today.

He also stood for courage and creativity. Many paintings, sculptures, and other kinds of art were created with his image.

The ancient Greeks were well-known for their beautiful pottery. It was often decorated with characters from myths, such as Pegasus. Examples of this pottery have lasted thousands of years. They are on display in museums all over the world.

Pegasus started out as a single character from Greek myths. But today his name is often used for any flying horse. People are still interested in Pegasus. They have even put him in movies. For instance, in the Disney movie *Hercules*, Pegasus is the hero's helper and best friend. Although his story in the movie is different than the one told by the ancient Greeks, it shows that the myth of Pegasus lives on.

Explore Online

Visit the website below. Does it give any new information about Pegasus that wasn't in Chapter Three?

Written in the Stars

abdocorelibrary.com/pegasus

LEGENDARY FACTS

Pegasus is a winged horse in Greek mythology.

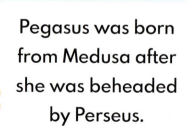

Pegasus was born from Medusa after she was beheaded by Perseus.

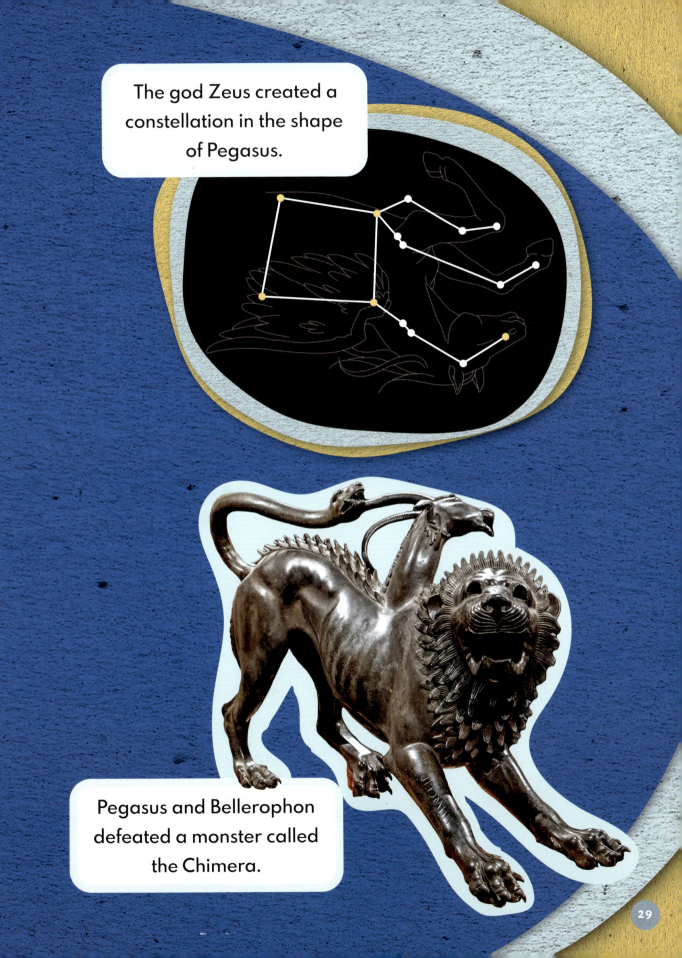

The god Zeus created a constellation in the shape of Pegasus.

Pegasus and Bellerophon defeated a monster called the Chimera.

Glossary

bridle
a harness that is placed on a horse's head and is used to control or guide the animal

civilization
a society that's organized and developed

constellation
a group of stars that form a pattern

fearsome
frightening in appearance

inspired
caused people to feel creative or do their best work

quest
a journey to do an important task

symbol
something that represents a certain quality or idea

Online Resources

To learn more about Pegasus, visit our free resource websites below.

Visit **abdocorelibrary.com** or scan this QR code for free Common Core resources for teachers and students, including vetted activities, multimedia, and booklinks, for deeper subject comprehension.

Visit **abdobooklinks.com** or scan this QR code for free additional online weblinks for further learning. These links are routinely monitored and updated to provide the most current information available.

Learn More

Bell, Samantha S. *Medusa*. Abdo, 2022.

Flynn, Sarah Wassner. *Greek Mythology*. National Geographic Kids, 2018.

Hudak, Heather C. *Poseidon*. Abdo, 2022.

Index

Athena, 17

Bellerophon, 6, 9, 16–18, 20, 24

Chimera, 7, 9, 17–18
constellation, 23–25

Hercules, 27
Hippocrene, 14

Lycia, 6–7

Medusa, 13–14, 21
Mount Helicon, 14
Mount Olympus, 18, 20
Muses, 14

Perseus, 13, 21
Poseidon, 13–14, 21
pottery, 26

quest, 6

temples, 11, 17

Zeus, 18, 20–21, 23

About the Author

Whitney Sanderson is the author of numerous books for young readers, including five in the historical fiction series *Horse Diaries* and two in the history series *Events that Changed America*. She lives with her family in Massachusetts.